THE BOOK OF CHOICE

"THE ROADMAP TO BETTER DOCUMENTATION AND PROCESS MAPPING"

POTSHA HARRIS

THE BOOK OF CHOICE
"THE ROADMAP TO BETTER DOCUMENTATION
AND PROCESS MAPPING"

iUniverse books may be ordered through booksellers or by contacting:

iUniverse
1663 Liberty Drive
Bloomington, IN 47403
www.iuniverse.com
844-349-9409

ISBN: 978-1-6632-1667-0 (sc)
ISBN: 978-1-6632-1666-3 (e)

Library of Congress Control Number: 2022922339

Print information available on the last page.

Printed in the United States of America.

iUniverse rev. date: 07/18/2023

ACKNOWLEDGEMENT

First and foremost, I thank God, my Heavenly Father, for giving me strength and endurance to complete this book. And a warm thank you to my family, friends, and supporters for their continuous encouragement and support.

To the following people who inspired me, provided support, and contributed to the development of this book: Geri Young-Duran, Najeeb Hatami, Jorge Marquez, Wardell Jones, Geraldine Smith, Richard Martin, Monique Rowen, Kimberly Locket, and Danielle Griffin.

I would like to thank my editors Janice Martin, LaWanda Harris, and Professor Elizabeth Kunnu for critiquing and editing the entire manuscript. You asked specific questions about the objective of the book and the audience that I wanted to capture. Your analysis of the book content gave me insight and assurance in the direction of simplification and efficiency. Thank you for all your hard work and dedication!

Thank you Della for your creative mind, patience, and knowledge of capturing what was important in designing the book cover.

CONTENTS

LIST OF TABLES

LIST OF FIGURES

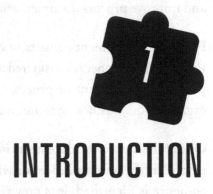

INTRODUCTION

Understanding Workflows, Business Process, Procedure Documentation

"Let's Go on a Journey"

Have you ever felt like you know your process but do not know how to put it into simple words? Who are the teams involved in the End-to-End (E2E) process?

We are on an expedition into the complexity of documentation through a simple journey of process mapping for the purpose of emerging the organization or customer's vision. Reading this book will assist you in successfully accomplishing your business goal(s) for implementing processes and reviewing your tools and systems in place.

The first step on this journey is to identify the discipline and why the process is being documented. It is imperative to remember, three attributes that play a major role in creating your documentation: people, process, and technology. First, focus on people and process followed by technology (tools and systems). In doing so, this will help to drive change and improve process documentation.

Process improvement consists of change(s). The Process Consultant or Process Practitioner is considered a 'Change Agent'. When implementing process improvement or process change, the change affects the entire organization, business systems, and all involved in the E2E process.

One of the most critical elements in the organization or customer journey is to identify your audience for which the process is created. Once the audience is identified, it is now time to brainstorm for ideas. The two most important components of writing a process or procedure are to identify the audience and understand the purpose. The Subject Matter Experts (SME) of both the consultant and the organization's disciplines will collaborate to determine each step in the E2E process.

There are several designs to customize your documentation. For the purpose of this book, the formats that will be discussed are step-by-step process, procedure, and work instruction. The illustrations of how the process will look, who will do the work, the time it takes to complete the work, and how it should be mapped out and implemented. It will assist the user to easily read, simplify, and understand the steps. The process diagram maps out each step and how it should be followed with a written collaboration table.

The process should be streamlined. So it is easily comprehended by both technical and non-technical staff.

Total Quality Management (TQM) is part of the Quality Assurance (QA) process. In providing TQM, it eliminates unnecessary steps, adds accuracy, and value. As the process is being developed, there should be an assigned person(s) or team to perform quality checks and testing.

PROCESS AND PROCEDURE DOCUMENTATION

2.1 WHAT IS PROCESS DOCUMENTATION

+ Process documentation is a method of writing to standardize a specific way to accomplish a task while working with cross-functional teams. Collaboration is important when writing and documenting business processes especially when teams are located globally.
+ Process documentation is a way to capture pertinent information to improve the business for growth and innovation. It is essential to review strengths, weaknesses, and opportunities within the process to continuously make improvements.

2.2 WHY DOCUMENT YOUR PROCESS

+ Documentation is necessary to avoid duplication and confusion in recording the process of your day-to-day responsibilities.

- It helps to understand what it takes to provide good customer service and maintain a profitable customer base.
- Customer Excellence is vital in maintaining the demand for products and services. Acknowledging the "Voice of the Customer" helps to provide improved customer satisfaction.

2.3 WHAT IS A PROCEDURE

- A document written to support a "Policy Directive". A Procedure is designed to describe who, what, where, when, why, and how for establishing corporate accountability in support of the implementation of a "policy" (Geckler, V., 2017, p 373).
- The "How" is further documented by each organizational unit in the form of "Work Instructions" which aims to further support a procedure by providing greater details (Geckler, V., 2017, p 373).

2.4 WHY DOCUMENT YOUR PROCEDURE

- It is important to document your procedure because it is a fixed, step-by-step sequence of activities and actions. In a procedure, a process can be part of the document and also can include different sections. It tells you more about the document. Various sections included in a procedure are the purpose, scope, entry inputs, and exit outputs. It also includes background information, acronyms, and definitions within the document. In addition, it includes different sign-offs from the teams involved and upper management prior to implementation.

UNDERSTANDING THE ORGANIZATION

3.1 UNDERSTAND THE GOALS AND OBJECTIVES

+ Understand the organization's goals and objectives. This is very important, so the writer can properly structure their thoughts and brainstorm.
+ Understand the driving force behind the mission statement.
+ Understand that the mission statement aligns with the business objective(s).
+ Unite the organization's mission, goal, and objective in a strategic alignment.
+ Understand the organization's short term and long term goal(s).
+ Understand the culture of the organization, its operation and alignment.
+ Know what compliance and standards the organization is following.
+ Maximize your resources, utilize your experience, and minimize waste. These things will prevent inefficient workflows, delivery wait time, and product error.

3.2 UNDERSTAND THE CUSTOMER OR ORGANIZATION REQUIREMENTS

+ Understand the work that is being requested.
+ Understand what it takes to provide excellent customer service.

    o Be a great listener and a friendly subject matter expert.

+ Align customer service with the clients' needs, wants, likes, and dislikes. This specific approach enhances the build-out of the process to develop documentation.
+ Tailor the documentation and process map based on the customer or the organization requirements.

3.3 UNDERSTANDING OF THE WORK THAT IS BEING REQUESTED

+ It is important to understand the requirements of the process. The customer looks to you as the SME for decision making concerning products and services.
+ The SME identifies open areas of needs that will improve performance.
+ Make sure it is understood upfront if the customer requirements are deliverable.
+ Understand the 'as is' (current state)' process in order to create the step-by-step, 'to be' (future state) process.

3.4 UNDERSTANDING THE TEAM IN PLACE TO EXECUTE THE WORK

+ Understand the skill sets of team members to correctly document your process and build your visual design. This is helpful with complex and complicated projects, as well as working with cross-functional global projects and teams.
+ Understand the structure of the team and how the team is set up. Example of a basic team structure consist of the executive

leadership, a trainer, a program manager, a process SME, an engineer, a tester, a business analyst, etc. These contributors are part of your technical and non-technical team.

+ Understand the SME day-to-day activities of cross-functional global team(s) in order to comply with specific compliance and regulations.

3.5 UNDERSTANDING HOW TO WORK WITH YOUR SME

+ It helps to have a 'to be' (current state) of the process in place whether written or visual. This will assist the SME when editing as oppose to trying to detail each step in round one.
+ Understand the jargon that is used in the area of expertise or the industry that the process documentation is being created.
+ Do a step-by-step walk through of the process with the SME.
+ Know the availability of the SME.
+ Make sure your completion timeline is aligned with the availability of the SME.

3.6 ASSIGNING ROLES AND RESPONSIBILITIES WITHIN THE E2E PROCESS

It is smart to assign the roles involved in the process. The use of the RACI chart is to identify roles and responsibilities. Listed below is the RACI Matrix that explains what a RACI is and what each letter of the acronym mean.

RACI Matrix - The RACI matrix is a responsibility assignment chart that maps out every task, milestone or key decision involved in completing a project and assigns which roles are **Responsible** for each action item, which personnel are **Accountable**, and, where appropriate, who needs to be **Consulted** or **Informed.** The acronym RACI stands for the four roles that stakeholders might play in any project.

- o A RACI matrix is the simplest, most effective means for defining and documenting project roles and responsibilities. Who is responsible, who is accountable, who needs to be consulted, and who must be kept informed at every step will improve your chances of project success. The RACI matrix is a visual account of actions and activities.

  - + **Responsible (R)** –People or stakeholders who do the work to achieve the task.
  - + **Accountable (A)** - Person or stakeholder who is the "owner" of the work.
    - o An accountable must sign off (approve) work that responsible provides. There is only one person accountable, which means that "the bucks stop there".
  - + **Consultant (C)** - People or stakeholders who need to give input before the work can be done and signed-off on. These people are "in the loop" and activate participants.
  - + **Informed (I)** – People or stakeholders who need to be kept "in the picture." They need updates on progress or decisions, but they do not need to be formally consulted, nor do they contribute directly to the task or decision (Kantor, 2018)

- ❖ RACI Scenario – Roles in the RACI are a major element of the E2E process showing the cross-functional teams involved in the step-by-step process with timelines included:

RACI Matrix Example: - **Customer Reconciliation Project**
- + Julie, Project Manager (PM) - Accountable
- + Healthcare Representative (HCR) – Consultant
- + Brad, Claims specialist (CS) - Responsible
- + John, Claims Manager (CM) – Informed
- + MMP, Claims System -Responsible

The reconciliation spreadsheet is emailed to the PM from the HCR for processing. The chart below provides key components, deliverables, activities, & timelines based on the role.

RACI MATRIC CHART ILLUSTRATION

RACI Definition
[R] Responsible - Those who do the work to achieve the task(s), others can be delegated to assist in the work required by the PM.
[A] Accountable - The one ultimately answerable for the correct and thorough completion of the deliverables and delegates the work to the responsible.
[C] Consulted - The person or team to be consulted prior to a final decision or action (2 way communication).
[I] Informed - The person or team in the loop throughout the process and told of the outcome after a decision is made (1 way communication).

Components	Activities	Timeline Tasks Completion	Healthcare Representative (HCR)	Project Manager (PM)	Claims Specialist (CS)	Claims Manager (CM)	MMP Claims System
			Roles				
Information Gathering	Healthcare Representative email Reconciliation Spreadsheet to claims manager	2 days	R	A	I	R	
	CM email claims reconciliation spreadsheet to CS	1 day	C	A	R	R	
	CS process claims based on HCR Provider Contract	3 days	I	A	R	I	R
	Claims are uploaded in the Claims Contract System	1 day	I	A	R	I	R
	Claims are processed based on the correct contract	1 day	I	A	R	C	R
Finalize Payment	Claims are processed EDI and paid through EFT	5 days	I	A	I	I	R
	Bulk check is sent EFT to HCR Provider Bank Account	1 day	I	A	R	I	R
	Confirmation of cashed check uploaded in Contract System	5 days	I	A	I	I	R

Figure 3. 1 - RACI Matric Chart Illustration

Before | During | After

How To Measure Your Process Success
Or
Is Your Process Successful?

BEFORE Designing the 'to be/future state' PROCESS

'as is' process

Review and outline 'as is' process with SME

Map-out your 'as is'

'as is' review completed and process mapped

'as is' process

DURING the Design of the 'to be' PROCESS

Build In QUality Checks

Design with current 'as is' steps

Design by streamlining the 'to be'

Design the 'to be' Lean

Remove unnecessary steps to reduce waste

Build In QUality Checks

AFTER the Design of the 'to be' PROCESS

'to be' Process design

1 Review developing 'to be' with SME

2 Make necessary updates or changes

3 Final review with Stakeholders

'to be' Process design

'future state' Process design

4 Make necessary updates or changes

5 Add measure criteria to establish success baseline

6 Confirm design and measure criteria's/ get final sign-off

'future state' Process design

'future state' Process design

7 Train and Implement completed 'future state' process

8 continuous improve your process (make updates yearly)

9 Train and Implement updated process

'future state' Process design

Figure 3. 2 - Process Measure, Before, During, and After Process Design

Document and build a concise, streamlined, collaborative process diagram

Review the 'as is' process, interview the subject matter experts, ask questions.

- Are all steps in the process necessary?
- Review each step of the 'as is' in order to map out the 'to be'.
- After the 'as is' is completed, take a second look to see what steps are necessary and what steps can be removed or combined.
- During the design of the 'to be', map the process lean, thus, making it efficient and effective.
- Assure the 'to be' is simplified to save time and money

Once the 'to be' process is completed, review with the SME's for changes and accuracy.

- The 'to be' process determines quality, speed, and value added to the customer.
- Eliminate unnecessary steps that are not measurable and involve waste.
- Test and measure the 'to be' process for accuracy and success. It should be tested and measured by using data to display KPIs'.

Upon completion of the 'to be' process, a policy and procedure for the new workflow should be created.

WRITING AND DOCUMENTING

The first thing to do when documenting the process or procedure is to understand the requirements of the process or procedure that is being implemented. A few things to know are listed below (who, what, where, when, why, and how):

1. Is this a new process or is this a re-engineering of an old process?
2. Is the process or procedure written based on specific compliance and standards?
3. Who is the target audience?
4. Who are the primary or required SME's involved in the task(s)?
5. Who are the Stakeholders and Teams involved in sign-off of the procedure or process?
6. What types of methodology used to define the 'as is' and the 'to be' process?

   ❖ (Six Sigma, Lean Six Sigma, DMAIC, TQM, etc)

7. Where is the process being implemented and the timeline of the delivery?
8. When is the process being implemented and how is it implemented?
9. Why is the process being created?

10. How to do the work? Outline the step-by-step E2E details of the process and sub-processes.

   ❖ Included in the E2E detail process flow are sub-processes that show other areas of the organization involved in the E2E.
   ❖ It is recommended to add callout's in your step by step process map to explain critical or vital steps in the process diagram and process documentation.
   ❖ It is recommended to highlight the steps in the process diagram that signifies critical or vital steps in the process.
   ❖ These are steps in the process that usually taking long cycle time to complete or road blocks.

11. Entry inputs and exit outputs are important elements of the procedure or process.

   ❖ Entry Inputs: Entry Inputs are prerequisite items that must be completed before the process can begin.
   ❖ Exit Outputs: Exit Outputs defines items that must be completed before the process can be concluded.

12. How do you measure the effectiveness of the process?

In the final step of the process documentation, it is important to measure the effectiveness. Measuring ensures the successful outcome of the process. In addition, testing and performing quality checks are critical elements for outcome success.

   ❖ The way to recognize the measurable outcome is by a percentage, a number, or a concept (data).
   ❖ Process mapping is a visual concept that describes how to design the process. This is where quality is built into the steps of the E2E. This is the 'check and balance' of the process.

❖ **Check and Balance** - Checks and balances are various procedures set in place to reduce mistakes and decrease risk (Beers, 2022).

The above list is a helpful guide for the user(s) to document the process. The main purpose is to assist the SME and stakeholders understand the effort.

MAPPING YOUR PROCESS

5.1 THINGS TO REMEMBER WHEN MAPPING THE PROCESS

a. Understand how to map the process using the right tools to create a step by step diagram.

b. It is important to know what type of process map to create based on the type of map that you want to develop. Also know what discipline will use the process map.

c. Use tools to define and demonstrate the process correctly.

d. It is better to use a process mapping tool rather than a substitute tool to create your process map.

e. Use a step-by-step graphical demonstration to show and explain each step of the process.

f. Number each step in the E2E process. It gives a clear vision of the start and end point in the process map.

g. Understand how to use data resources to map and define the process.

h. Flexibility is key in order to be consistent with the customer's mapping tool.

i. Work effectively with the SME to identify the step-by-step process.

Below are suggested tools that are beneficial to create process maps and diagraming workflows. There are others tools that may not be listed.

5.2 VARIOUS DIAGRAMING TOOLS USED TO MAP OUT YOUR PROCESS

a) Microsoft Visio
b) Miro Collaboration Tool
c) Smartdraw
d) Edraw Max
e) LucidChart
f) Cacoo
g) Textografo
h) ConceptDraw Diagram

The tools above provide the right elements to effectively map your process steps. Process mapping is a journey and storytelling design, therefore, it must be created so the reader is able to follow the details of each task and activity. A visual picture is easier to comprehend.

Key steps in implementing the process: train the organization communities, explain what is a process flow, and how to design a process map. It is essential to allow the process map to tell the story, help the user quickly grasp next steps and understand the different graphical boxes. A suggestion is to number each step of the process diagram to align with your detailed Process Collaboration Table; so when you are explaining the process flow, both match.

Document and build concise streamlined process map

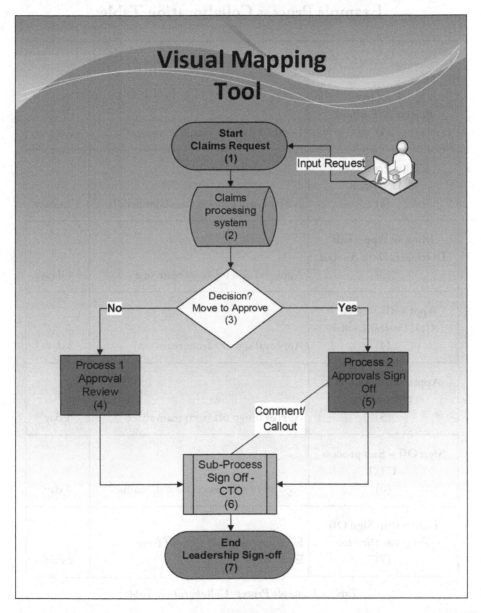

Figure 5. 1 - Example Process Map

Example Process Collaboration Table

Tasks/SME | Activities | Timeline to complete Activities		
Let Go *Process Consultant,* (1)	Let the Process Consultant move	2 days
Claim Processed *AAF System* (2)	AAF system process the claim details	9-14 days
Move to Approval? *Developer, Data Analyst* (3)	Approval sign off from team one	4 days
Approvals Review 1 *Ops, Process Leader* (4)	Approval sign off from team two	3 days
Approvals Sign Off 2 *QA Leader* (5)	Approval sign off from team three	1 day
Sign Off – Sub process *CTO* (6)	Sign off of sub-process for all teams	1 day
Leadership Sign Off *Program Director* (7)	Final approval and sign-off from leadership	2 days

Table 1 Example Process Collaboration Table

DEVELOPING YOUR PROCESS DOCUMENTATION

6.1 IS THIS A NEW PROCESS?

a. Define the purpose and scope of the new process.
b. Gather data and requirements that are applicable to the process at hand.
c. Make sure the right tools are used to complete the process map.
d. Understand the customer goals and objectives.
e. Understand the audience.
f. Know how much time that is required to complete the process.
g. Making sure the process is lean and error free.
h. Take out the waste and include value added to the customer.
i. List the resources needed to complete the process.
j. The process should be measurable using Key Performance Indicators (KPIs').

     ✦   This method is data driven.

k. Who are the final sign-offs and who will be responsible for enforcing the process?

6.2   IS THIS AN EXISTING PROCESS (RE-ENGINEERED PROCESS)?

a.   Update requirements that are applicable to the process at hand.

b.   Understand areas that need to be updated in the process.

c.   Make the process lean, take out waste, include added value to the customer, and make it error free.

d.   Did the client requirements change to achieve their goal(s)?

e.   Is the audience the same?

f.   Know how much time that is required to complete the process.

g.   List the resources needed to complete the process.

h.   The process should be measurable using Key Performance Indicators (KPIs').

   •   This method is data driven.

i.   Who are the final sign-offs and who will be responsible for enforcing the process?

TRAINING AND IMPLEMENTATION

7.1 TRAINING AND IMPLEMENTING YOUR PROCESS

Training is utmost important to the end user. In order for it to be operational, the trainer avoids complicated scenarios. The training material is of great value to the end user.

A. There must be a responsible person from upper management or leadership to make sure the process is enforced.

B. Training should be specific to the process that is provided to the end user. There are many ways to implement training. Below are types of training offerings to consider:

- Instructor Led (hands on)
- Virtual real-time
- Live Sandbox
- Computer base
- e-Learning (web-based)
- User Guide
- Implementation Guide
- Train the Trainer

CONTINUOUS IMPROVEMENT AND TRAINING

Functional assignments and Continuous improvement discussions are the final steps in documenting, updating, maintaining, and improving your processes.

A critical part of the E2E process is the assignment of roles and responsibilities of the cross-functional team.

Continuous Improvement is an ongoing effort to improve products, processes, or services by reducing waste, increasing quality, and adding value. This continuous effort drives a competitive advantage for the organization.

Below are things to consider in the development of a continuous improvement plan or program.

a. Training is a vital part of continuous improvement. The staff must understand the process in order to be successful.
b. Maintain the customer database to gather Key Performance Indicators (KPI's) as it relates to opportunities, problems, or improvement. The customer database is important to capture relevant data.

c. Your processes and procedures should be updated a minimal of every six months (6) or yearly if applicable.

d. Train staff at least twice a year on new or updated processes and procedures.

CONCLUSION

Now that we have completed our expedition, we now understand how documentation can be simple in process mapping. Customer satisfaction is significant in measuring organizational growth and return on investment (ROI) in this journey.

Once the process is mapped out, tracking and removing waste within the E2E becomes easier to assess for value added.

Defined below are methodologies to consider when documenting your process and data capturing. These methodologies help eliminate waste and measure the success of the processing defining benefits:

- **Six Sigma** is a data-driven methodology that provides tools and techniques to define and evaluate each step of a process. It provides methods to improve efficiencies in a business structure, improve the quality of the process and increase the bottom-line profit (What is six Signma?, 2020).

  o Six Sigma is a quality-control process that business use to eliminate defects and improve processes (Hayes, Six Sigma, 2022).

- **Lean Six Sigma** is a team-focused managerial approach that seeks to improve performance by eliminating waste and defects. It combines Six Sigma methods and tools and the lean manufacturing-lean enterprise philosophy, striving to eliminate waste of physical resources, time, effort, and talent while assuring quality in production and organizational processes. Under the tenets of Lean Six Sigma any use of resources that do not create <u>value</u> for the end customer is considered a waste and should be eliminated (Kenton, Lean Six Sigma, 2021).

- o **Lean** focuses on non-value added and waste reduction.
- o **Lean** seeks to eliminate and address inefficiencies your process flow by identifying causes of problems and developing solutions to address them (Kenton, Lean Six Sigma, 2021).

- **DMAIC Methodology** (Define, Measure, Analyze, Improve, Control) Used when an organization is improving its existing processes during a process improvement project. The heart of DMAIC is making continuous improvements to an existing process through objective problem solving (Six Sigma Fundamentals: What is DMAIC?, 2014).

- o **DMAIC** is used primarily for improving existing business processes (What is six Sigma?, 2020).

GLOSSARY: ACRONYMS AND DEFINITIONS

ACRONYMS

- CLSSBB: Certified Lean Six Sigma Black Belt
- CSSGB: Certified Six Sigma Green Belt
- E2E: End-to-End
- DMAIC: Define, Measure, Analyze, Improve, Control
- ITIL: Information Technology Infrastructure Library
- KPI's: Key Performance Indicators
- QA: Quality Assurance
- SME: Subject Matter Expert
- RACI: Responsible, Accountable, Consultant, Informed
- TQM: Total Quality Management

DEFINITIONS

- **End to End Process (E2E)** – Describes a process that takes a system or service from beginning to end and delivers a complete functional solution (Kenton, End-to-End, 2022).

- **End User** - The ultimate consumer of a finished product (Top Lookups Right Now, n.d.).

- **Procedure** – A set of actions that is the official or accepted way of doing something. (Dictionaries, n.d.).
    - A Fixed, step-by-step sequence of activities or course of action (with definite start and end points) that must be followed in the same order to correctly perform a task or tasks (Dictionaries, n.d.).

- **Process** - A series of actions or steps taken in order to achieve a particular result. (Dictionaries, n.d.).

- **Subject Matter Expert (SME)** – Is an individual with a deep understanding of a particular job, process, department, function, technology, machine, material, or type of equipment (Reh, 2020).

- **Total Quality Management (TQM)** - Describes a management approach to long-term success through customer satisfaction. In a TQM effort, all members of an organization participate in improving processes, products, services, and the culture in which they work (WHAT IS TOTAL QUALITY MANAGEMENT (TQM)?, n.d.).

- **Work Instructions** - A description of the specific tasks and activities within an organization; generally, outline all of the different jobs needed for the operation in great detail and is a key element to running the operation smoothly (Quality Documentation Erga HR Site- Documents Types, n.d.).

APPENDICES - 7

The following artifacts are included in this document:

1. APPENDIX A: Flowchart Symbols and Their Meanings
2. APPENDIX B: A Tool Kit on Developing your content
3. APPENDIX C: Information to consider when developing your documentation
4. APPENDIX D: Process Collaboration Table
5. APPENDIX E: High level Overview diagrams
6. APPENDIX F: Detailed Process Flow diagrams
7. APPENDIX G: RACI Matrix Chart Illustration

Appendix A

FLOWCHART BASIC SYMBOLS AND THEIR MEANINGS:

5 BASIC FLOWCHART SYMBOLS

Various flowchart shapes are used for drawing different types of flowcharts. Each flowchart symbol has its own meaning and context where it is used appropriately. However, whether you want to read a flowchart or try to make one by yourself, knowing the common symbols and what they represent will make things easier. Here, you will see the five flowchart symbols that are very popular and commonly used in almost every flowchart (Flowchart Symbols and Their Usage, n.d.).

Symbol	Name	Function
	Start/end	An oval represents a start or end point
→	Arrows	A line is a connector that shows relationships between the representative shapes
	Input/Output	A parallelogram represents input or output
	Process	A rectagle represents a process
	Decision	A diamond indicates a decision

Figure 1 - Basic Flowchart Symbols, (Flowchart Symbols, n.d.)

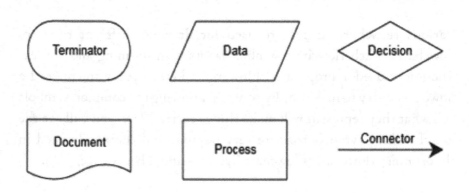

Figure 2- Basic Flowchart Symbols, (Grapholite Flow Charts, n.d.)

Appendix B

TOOL KIT TO DEVELOP YOUR CONTENT AND PROCESS DIAGRAM

i. Basic Diagram Tool – Map out the step-by-step process

ii. Brainstorming Tools - Organize your thoughts to document and diagram the process.

iii. Imaging Tool – Capture screenshots of how the process will look

iv. Capturing Data Tool – Utilize for building your data to show your outcome

v. Documenting or Writing Tool – Capture your content in the most effective way

Appendix C

INFORMATION TO CONSIDER WHEN DEVELOPING YOUR DOCUMENTATION

Below are elements to consider when developing the procedure and/or process.

- Purpose
- Scope
- Resources used to document the procedure and/or process.
- Acronyms that are in the procedure and/or process.
- Definitions that apply to the procedure and/or process.
- Background Information - After choosing a topic, locate introductory sources that give *basic background information* about the subject. Finding background information at the beginning of your research is especially important.
- Roles and Responsibilities – List the people involved in the process and the role that each person play in completing specific task(s).
- Create a high - level overview diagram
- Entry Scenario – Defines how the procedure is used to support the process.
- Entry Inputs – How the procedure and/or process starts.
- Exit Outputs – How the procedure and/or process ends.
- Create a detailed procedure flow diagram

- Create a task, SME, activities, and timeline process collaboration table
- Measures – The successful outcome of the procedure and/or process.
- References – Specific guidelines used to write the procedure and/or process.
- Revision and change History – The revision or change history is dated when the document is updated.
- Maintenance – How will the document be maintained?
- Approval Signatures – The approval signature is defined as the person(s) responsible for approving the documentation.
- Appendix or Attachments – Any artifacts, charts, table, diagrams, policies, procedures, specific work instructions, etc, used to help understand the procedure and/or process.

Appendix D

EXAMPLE: PROCESS COLLABORATION TABLE

Tasks/SME	Activities	Timeline

Table 2 - Process Collaboration Table

Appendix E

PROCEDURE FLOW CHARTS, HIGH LEVEL OVERVIEW DIAGRAMS AND DETAILED DIAGRAMS

FLOW CHARTS

What is a flow chart: A flowchart is a graphical description of a process or algorithm using various symbols of different forms to represent operations, data, threads, etc. relations between which are shown by the arrows? Flowcharts are used to explain sophisticated ideas in a simplified manner so that even inexperienced audience can easily get the idea. Flowcharts are also helpful to their creators — when developing a flowchart, you visually break a process to steps and begin to clearly understand the step's place as a part of the process as a whole.

Why use flowcharts: Flowcharts will help you understand how logical the process is, discover problem areas and relations breaks, define the complexity of a process, and create a common knowledge base for a process.

Flowcharts are commonly used to:

+ document and describe the existing process;
+ develop modification to the existing process or research where the problems may arise;
+ develop an absolutely new process;
+ define how, where and when to measure the existing process in order to make sure it corresponds to the requirements (Grapholite Flow Charts, n.d.)

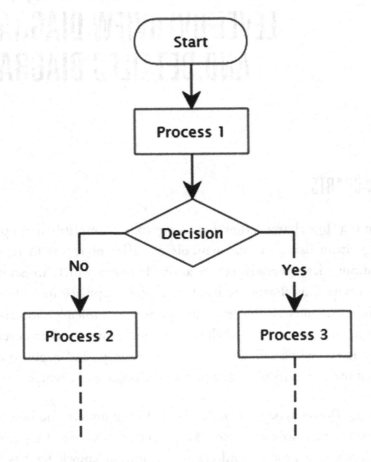

Figure 3 – Flowchart, (Grapholite Flow Charts, n.d.)

High Level Overview Diagram

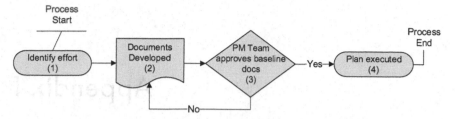

Figure 4 - High Level Overview Diagram (1)

High Level Overview Diagram

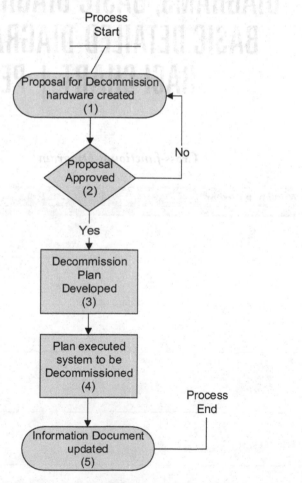

Figure 5 - High Level Overview Diagram (2)

Appendix F

CROSS-FUNCTIONAL PROCESS DIAGRAMS, BASIC DIAGRAM, AND BASIC DETAILED DIAGRAM WITH RACI CHART | PERSONAS'

Cross-functional Diagram

Training and Workshop Review	
Technical Service	
Customer Service	
Training Lead	
Documentation SME	
Management	

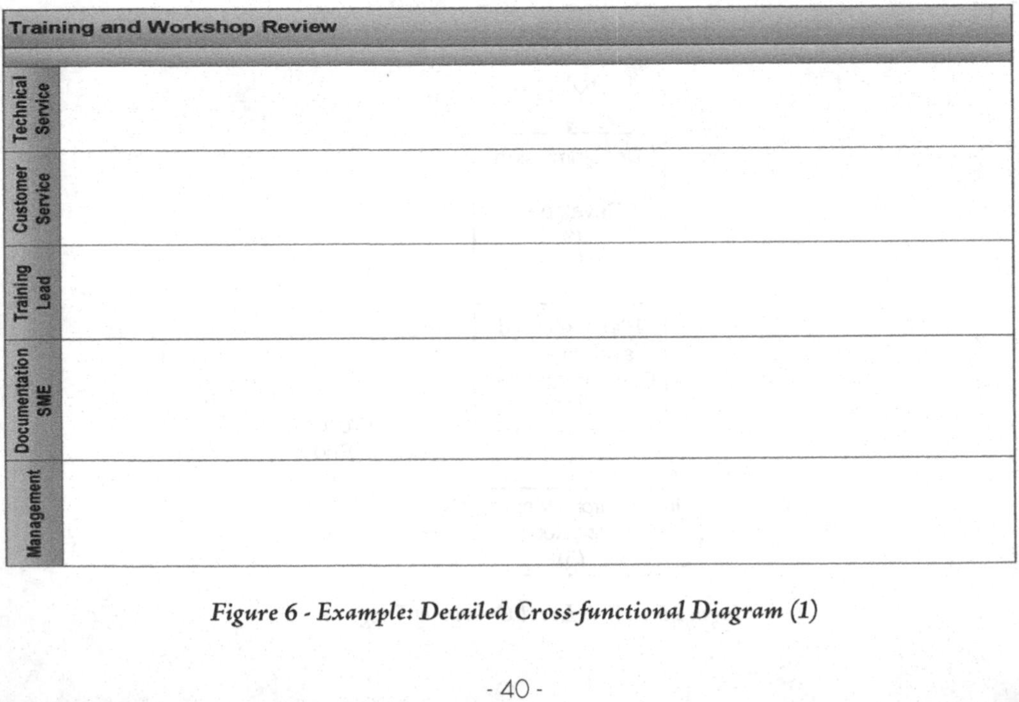

Figure 6 - Example: Detailed Cross-functional Diagram (1)

Cross-functional Detailed Workflow Diagram

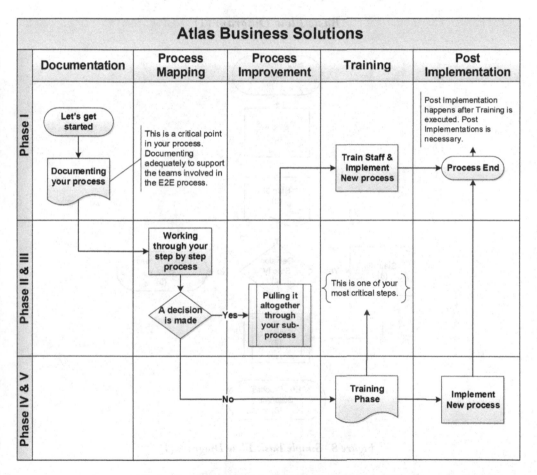

Figure 7 - Cross-functional Workflow Diagram (2)

Basic Flow Diagram (1)

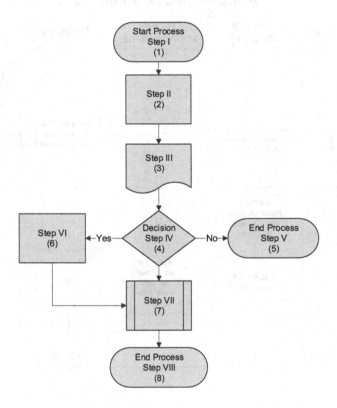

Figure 8 - Simple Basic Flow Diagram (1)

Basic Flow Cross-functional Diagram with
RACI and Personas' included (2)

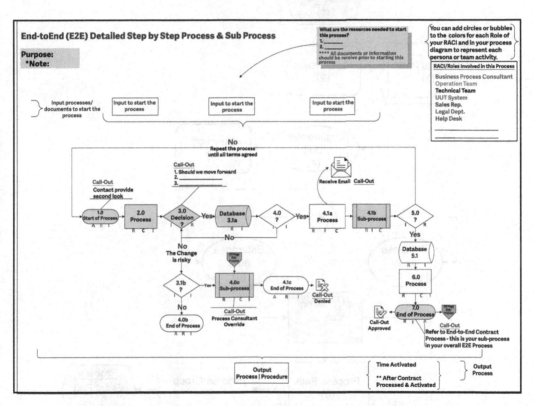

Figure 9 - Basic Detailed Cross-functional Diagram with RACI and Personas' (2)

Event-Driven Process Chain (EPC) Diagrams (1)

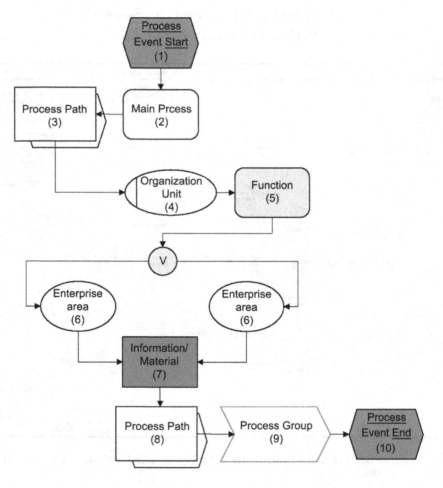

Figure 10 - Event- Driven Process Chain (EPC) Diagram – (1)

Event-Driven Process Chain (EPC) Diagrams (2)

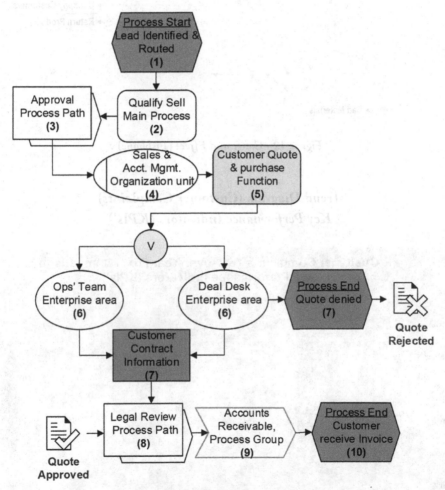

Figure 11- Event- Driven Process Chain (EPC) Diagram – (2)

Cause and Effect Diagram (Fishbone)

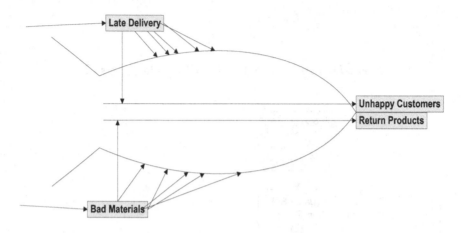

Figure 12 - Cause and Effect (Fishbone)

Trend Diagram (Customer Complaints)
Key Performance Indicators (KPIs')

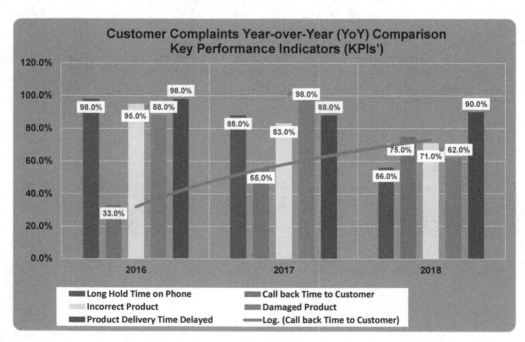

Figure 13 - Trend Customer Complaints Diagram

Appendix G

EXAMPLE: RACI CHART ILLUSTRATION

RACI CHART EXAMPLE

RACI Definition
[R] Responsible - Those who do the work to achieve the task(s), others can be delegated to assist in the work required by the PM.
[A] Accountable - The one ultimately answerable for the correct and thorough completion of the deliverables and delegates the work to the responsible.
[C] Consulted - The person or team who need to give input before the work is completed or signed-off on (2 way communication).
[I] Informed - The person or team who is kept in the loop on progress and told of the outcome after a decision is made (1 way communication).

Components	Activities	Roles				
		Time Task Completed	Project Manager	Process SME	Customer Service	MPP Payment System
Information Gathering	Work with team to pay customer	2 days	A	R	C	R
Finalize Payment	Customer received Invoice	1 hour	A	I	R	R

Figure 14 - RACI Chart Illustration

REFERENCES

Beers, B. (2022, March 22). *Checks and Balance*. Retrieved August 13, 2020, from Investopedia: https://www.investopedia.com/terms/c/checks-and-balances.asp

Dictionaries. (n.d.). Retrieved August 13, 2022, from Dictionary Cambridge: https://dictionary.cambridge.org/us/dictionary/

Flowchart Symbols. (n.d.). Retrieved August 25, 2022, from Smartdraw: https://www.smartdraw.com/flowchart/flowchart-symbols.htm

Flowchart Symbols and Their Usage. (n.d.). Retrieved July 26, 2018, from Edraw: https://www.edrawsoft.com/flowchart-symbols.html

Geckler, V. M. (2017). Procedures Should be Compliant to the Regulation. In V. M. Geckler, *Design Controls, Risk Management & Process Validation for Medical Device Professionasl* (1ˢᵗ ed., p. 373). Wasatch Consulting Resources LLC. Retrieved October 19, 2022, from https://www.google.com/books/edition/DESIGN_CONTROLS_RISK_MANAGEMENT_PROCESS/SnCLDwAAQBAJ?hl=en&gbpv=1&printsec=frontcover

Grapholite Flow Charts. (n.d.). Retrieved July 26, 2018, from Grapholite: https://grapholite.com/Diagrams/FlowCharts

Hayes, A. (2022, May 1). *Six Sigma*. Retrieved August 12, 2021, from Investopedia: https://www.investopedia.com/terms/s/six-sigma.asp

Kantor, B. (2018, January 30). *The RACI matrix: Your blueprint for project success.* Retrieved August 13, 2020, from CIO: https://www.cio.com/article/287088/project-management-how-to-design-a-successful-raci-project-plan.html

Kenton, W. (2021, March 30). *Lean Six Sigma.* Retrieved August 13, 2021, from Investopedia: https://www.investopedia.com/terms/l/lean-six-sigma.asp

Kenton, W. (2022, May 24). *End-to-End.* Retrieved August 13, 2020, from Investopedia: https://www.investopedia.com/terms/e/end-to-end.asp

Quality Documentation Erga HR Site- Documents Types. (n.d.). Retrieved September 20, 2022, from erga: https://ierga.com/hr/quality-management/quality-documentation/

Reh, J. (2020, July 17). *What Is a Subject Matter Expert?* Retrieved August 13, 2021, from The Balance Careers: https://www.thebalancecareers.com/subject-matter-expert-2275099

Six Sigma Fundamentals: What is DMAIC? (2014, August 13). Retrieved August 12, 2020, from Six Sigma Daily: https://www.sixsigmadaily.com/six-sigma-fundamentals-dmaic/

Top Lookup Right Now. (n.d.). Retrieved August 13, 2022, from Merriam-Webster: https://www.merriam-webster.com/

What is six Sigma? (2020, January 9). Retrieved August 13, 2020, from Six Sigma Daily: https://www.sixsigmadaily.com/what-is-six-sigma/

WHAT IS TOTAL QUALITY MANAGEMENT (TQM)? (n.d.). Retrieved August 13, 2020, from ASQ: https://asq.org/quality-resources/total-quality-management

Printed in the United States
by Baker & Taylor Publisher Services